Crown of Thorms

G W Colkitto

Published by Cinnamon Press
Office 49019, PO Box 92, Cardiff, CF11 1NB.
www.cinnamonpress.com

The right of G W Colkitto to be identified as author of this work has been asserted by him in accordance with the Copyright, Designs and Patent Act, 1988. © 2021, G W Colkitto.

ISBN 978-1-78864-149-4

British Library Cataloguing in Publication Data. A CIP record for this book can be obtained from the British Library.

Designed and typeset in Bodoni by Cinnamon Press. Cover design by Adam Craig.

Cinnamon Press is represented by Inpress Ltd.

Acknowledgements

Thanks to the editors who have published some of the poems in the is collection. 'Not Sonnet No 2' appeared in *Burn and Rave;* 'Not Sonnet No 3', 'a chancer's hope' & 'a lady's wish were published by Hybriddreich.

I am indebted to Jan Fortune for her editorial assistance and support and to Adam Craig for the cover design.

Author biography

G. W. Colkitto is a widely published poet, short story writer and novelist from Paisley. He won the Scottish Writers Short Story Competition, in 2011, and the Scottish Writers Poetry Competition in 2012. His poetry collection, The Year of the Loch, was published by Diehard Press, in 2017; a second collection, Waitin tae Meet wi the Deil was published by Diehard 2018. He is also the creator of Sebastian Symes, Victorian Detective. His previous pamphlets with Cinnamon Press are *Brantwood — The Place of Little Green Poems* and *Clyde: my river,* plus the full length poetry collection, *Shake the Kaleidoscope.*

Contents

With Power comes betrayal

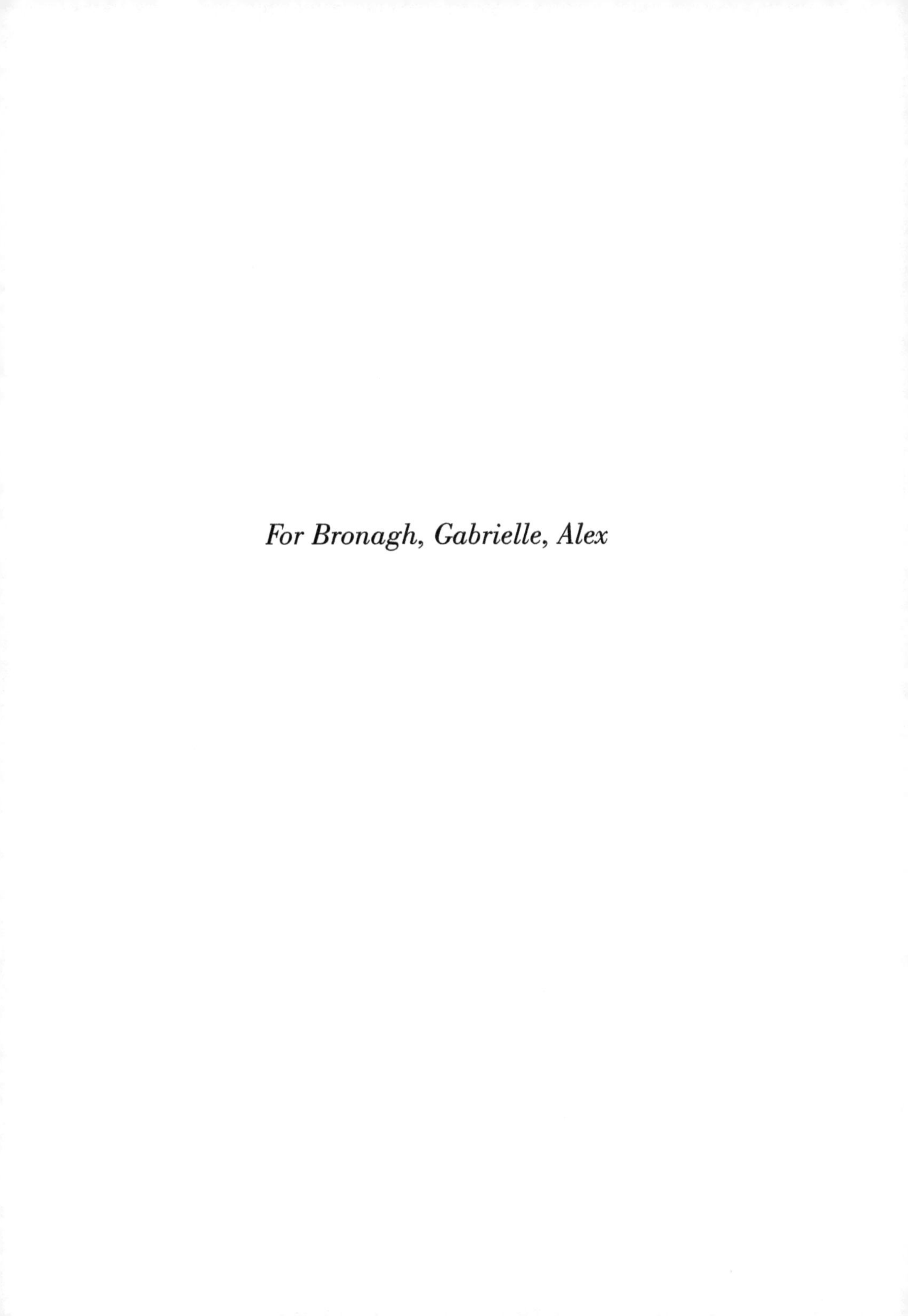

For Bronagh, Gabrielle, Alex

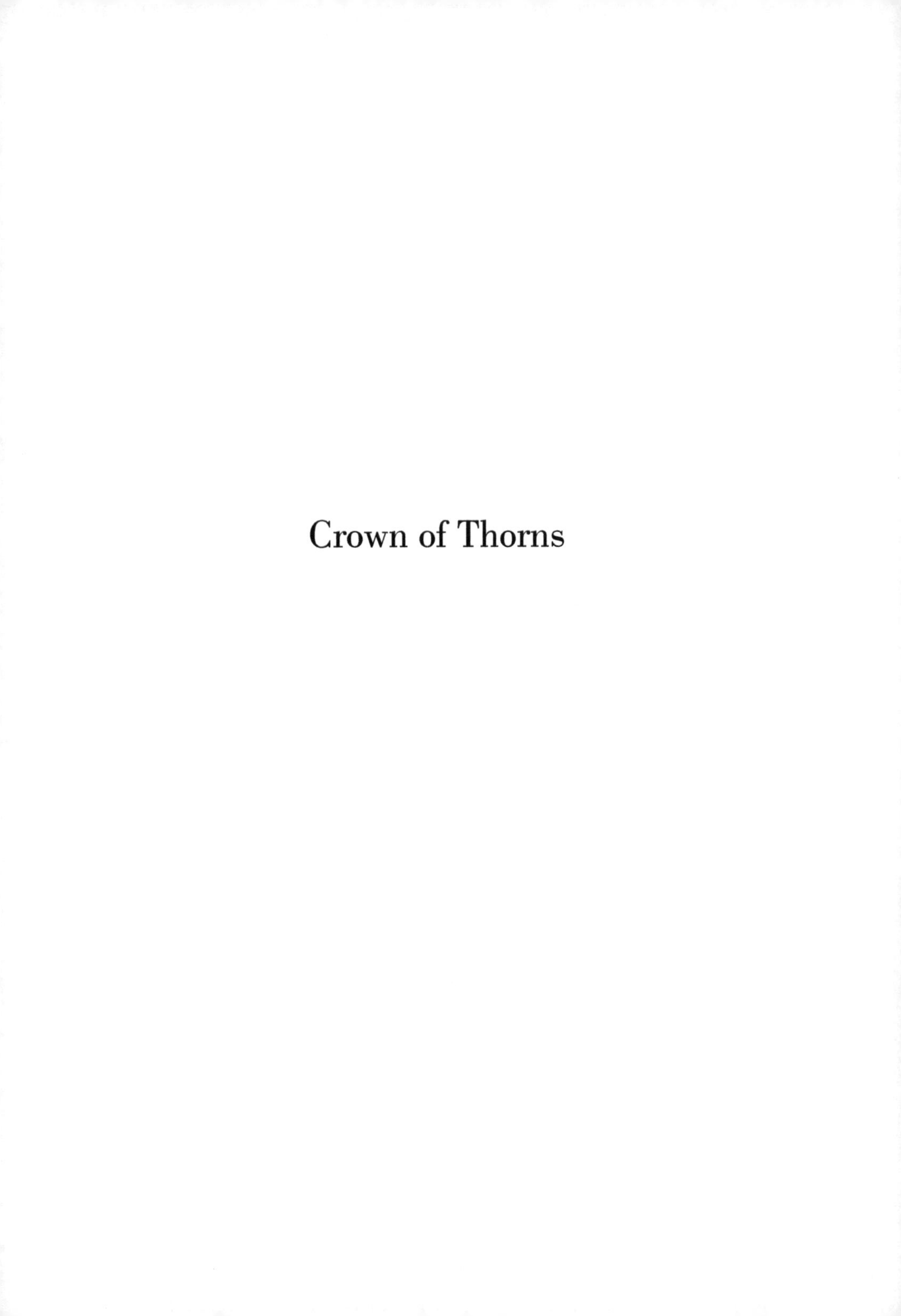

Crown of Thorns

To those who call poems sonnets

Not Sonnet No 1

I have a need to write does that sound trite
one of those named thingies you know like Shakespeare
but without those tight rules on rhythm and line length nor
some scheme of rhyme I mean have I world enough or time
for that palaver I'll grab the modern freedom to chuck such malarkey
but take the name for the gravity and listen this ones good because
I say it will be fourteen lines and I can claim it is the first perhaps
I'll write a sequence and have some lines repeat it will save time
thinking up another set to fit inside the framework of this page
it is intended to have this shape. I want you to gape in awe
there I've let that slip but I know you'll understand and anyway
bugger I might go back and change a word or two for these are getting
out of hand. Still let the flow carry me on and as fortune frames the farce
as that old codger Chaucer said of old I'll keep bold and have you

Not Sonnet No 2

as that old codger Chaucer said of old I'll keep it bold and have you
for a fool like all l want to stamp under foot not give a hoot
for your pain or sorrow debris is what I seek there are no rules
for me but fourteen lines demands attention so I can brag
I am master and you the knave my talent gives me rights
no wrongs exist in my vocabulary so sodding hear me out
stamp up your foothills to my heights where I stare down
I love the sight of weeping gnashing teeth oh how I pray for tears
a nasty word so brighter than the kind no honeyed phrases
taste as sweet as those bitter jibes I throw from my Olympus
my darting tongue licks you into the spit of envy
do not deny you have been counting hoping I would forget
but this is the way I hold your bleeding heart see fourteen
on the line the laugh is mine my genius does not

Not Sonnet No 3

on the line the laugh is mine my genius does not
countenance rebuke and if I say it is so then I
expect your homage to be absolute I am resolute
in liking this form even if I fail to have it rhyme
why these are—ittonian and valid as Petrarchan
or Shakespearean or any other ian, paul or jim
who pontificates on how my life is spent or coyly
suggests at a crime suggests I'm in the wrong
look I'll put in a change of note here in the ninth
line just to show I know your dictates and could
make the poems fit but why for I do not
consider it a scheme for today though as I say
it rolls off the tongue and impresses the listener
and this is a sonnet not just a poem of fourteen

Not Sonnet No 4

and this is a sonnet not just a poem of fourteen
random conjured thoughts believe me there is depth
and width and maybe heights in every line
it holds time and line and finely expresses well
it is up to you to find what is planted on the page to grow
so go with the flow and be swept along on a tide of wonder
pulled asunder by the power of each weighted phrase
come dance upon a pin and sing of the new Jerusalem
for God and man so net days' passing follies
trapped in the tram lines I speed on and upwards and
beyond into the spaces and the silences damned
for in truth I'd leave it here but I have a desire
for one of those named thingies you know like Shakespeare
which I have a need to write does that sound trite

For Lost Love

To be alone

And ever do I know that it is so,
I do not doubt that happiness was ours.
We built a castle, looked out from its towers
at those who ploughed and scattered far below,
and never did we contemplate a fall,
that our stone battlement might crumble,
that in those wastelands we might stumble,
in blindness there with no protecting wall.
What kindly place will shelter from life's blast,
what kist o'er which to pull a leaden stone,
I seek a cell where I may weep alone,
dark as the night, now that my love is past.
I do not want your care your sympathy.
I do not want your tears your empathy.

I do not want

I do not want your tears your empathy.
You do not see what lingers in my head.
You do not know the things undone, unsaid,
unless you are cursed with telepathy
and hear those words I shouted in a rage,
have seen the callous laugh, the crafted smile,
have watched me turn on charm to beguile
the failings I have hidden from front stage,
secreted in the wings but always there.
This tragedy I play out matters not.
I wrote the script, I crafted every plot.
My punishment is just, the verdict fair.
He, who sings out loud and out of tune,
is but a shallow man, a base poltroon.

A Shallow Man

Is but a shallow man, a base poltroon,
who makes of love a slave to his self will,
holds it so tight his harsh embrace does kill
the freshness, and with lustre tarnished, soon
hides it away, pretends it still is bright.
His rusted hulk deserves no saddened eye.
His castle bleak, his self indulgent sigh,
is but acknowledgement the dying light
is consequence of his own foolishness.
His understanding, weak, has come too late.
No outstretched hand can save him from his fate.
I did not know when I had happiness,
I therefore ask no-one to weep for me,
clarity came slow, but, at last, I see.

At Last I See

Clarity came slow, but, at last, I see
the fault lines running north to south within.
The fissures and the caverns 'neath ageing skin
define the way I am, the actual me,
not whom I show, pretending that I am,
and when I bought the dream, pranced on the stage,
the empty words I scribbled on the page
were emperor's clothes, mirror for the sham.
But yet in all the selfishness I brought,
your open heart, your honesty and love,
your laugh, your joy, your placing all above
any selfish act, any selfish thought,
love lifted high and also laid us low,
and ever do I know that it is so.

I heard a scientist say that the questions to ask are How? for Why? often has no answer

You should be Sixty.

'We know the how, but not the why,' such truth
in those few words I hear. I learned that Ruth
toiled for another, but why did God,
if God is good, demand of her that load,
or test out Job, or Samson blind, or ask
me to accept in faith that hardest task,
to bury one whose death tore out my heart;
my world ending. Why choose the brighter part
and leave the dull, the wicked, and the cruel.
If not a God, it is the Fates that rule,
threads severed on a whim, a random choice.
No prayer, no hymn of praise, no angel voice,
can intercede, and I, who know the how,
can only shout out why? I shout it now.

*

I shout it now, why do the powerful fall
into that depth which wishes to destroy, all
who question the wisdom of their thinking
and, by their might, will crush, without blinking,
the child, the poor, the innocent, to dust,
uncaring sacrifice to selfish lust.
They strut and posture, vilify and rage,
their position, their place upon the stage,
is theirs by right. Such twisted ego strives
to say it is more precious than those lives.
How strange to wish to stand in history,
etch in the blood and gore of victory,
as one who little thought what victory cost,
for power, once gained, must not be lost.

*

Must not be lost, for somewhere must be love.
Must not be lost, for somehow I will love
again. Despots also die and no-one cries
for them, as I cry for you. My heart flies,
for fates and Gods cannot destroy what I
have locked away. In me you never die
and I still see you smile and hear you laugh.
It is not all I wish, but is enough
to let the sunlight dapple in my soul,
to bind the broken parts into a whole.
If it is the fates, or be it God, it
matters not. You and I will always sit
all powerful in the love. which binds us both.
'I know not how, I know not why.' Such truth.

Glasgow West End

Down Byres Road—

Passing Fancy

And here a couple are drinking herbal teas
discuss the wine to have with venison
their climate change debate goes on and on
the intellect of Glasgow takes its ease
a student hurries by with worried frown
he's lost the notes he made on Wittgenstein
and racks his brain for everywhere he's been
can he recall the points that he wrote down
a Chihuahua barks from a Gucci bag
blaring traffic horns seem to answer back
grey clouds gather with an approaching squall
into the air a voice cries—nag nag nag
how quickly this bright day is turning dark
in the cafe the youth feels rather small

Fill yer plate

in the cafe the youth feels rather small
his companion orders him Simnel cake
smugly adds it's not named for the fake
fake what he says I dinnae can recall
she laughs oh it's ancient history now
you've enough to learn without more silly facts
don't look so hurt we came here to relax
tell me again what is this stupid row
he sighs its yon woman cross the landing
ye'd think she wis some bluidy royalty
wrinkles up her nose as if I'm excrement
sma-est thing anither misunderstanding
an she's haun in glove wie the Faculty
yon missus from thae West-end tenements

A chancer's hope

Oh, misses, from thae West-end tenements
doon Byres Road, I watch ye strut and sway
wi clickin heels an smellin o Gerlais
ye giggle, shimmie, seekin compliments.
Of course, I ken it's never yer intent
tae pull the likes o me, nae way hosay.
I bet ye've wondered whit it's like tae play
wi bits o rough, ye dinna look content,
sae come tae me an I will strip ye bare,
I'll slap they firm ripe cheeks, an make ye squeal,
aw they dark dreams and lusts I'll satisfy,
wan night wi me an ye'll be back for mair,
ye'll realise that passion can be real
ye have tae find it oot before ye die.

A lady's wish (Byres Road)

You have to find it out before you die
if you can tame the roughest of the street,
with sex all things are yours, is not a lie,
and many gifts are lavished at your feet
but you would have men grovel for your kiss,
both rich and poor, the handsome and the geek
so dazzled by your body, they dismiss
all thoughts that they are putty, victim, weak,
unequal in this game of lust and power,
so that their metal crumbles in your hands,
their manhood broken by a woman's glower
and them unfit to live with your demands.
Man the hunter finds he's but the chancer,
prey to your seductive necromancer.

Prowling Lothario

Prey to your seductive necromancer
that matriarch ahead is svelte and trim.
Clarinda, Archimedes, and plane Jim,
her three grandchildren cavort and pester
with daft questions, which she cannot answer.
Praising the children is the way to win
her to your cause, and then be ripe for sin.
Time to overtake by strolling faster,
compliment her brood, flash your famous smile,
jacket open to show Yves St Laurent.
Suggest a night of culture with a play
in Oran Mhor, then flirting for a while,
Madame, you fill my heart and soul with song
I beg you to say yes and make my day.

Dowanhill Matriarch

I beg you to say yes and make my day.
A nod, a smile, she checks his calf-skin shoes
the silver headed cane, a man to choose
for an exciting fling, for he will pay
what she desires, she'll only have to say
a diamond ring, a trip to where Toulouse
Lautrec once roamed, from Sacre Coeur the views
will be worth this charmer's sinful way.
Her husband, Jim, a boring architect,
is happy with his church and golfing mates,
she'll tell him she is singing in a choir,
will serve him right for the years of neglect.
Candle-lit dinners, romantic sensuous dates,
is this the man to re-alight her fire?

Aphrodite drinks in The Curlers

Is this the man to re-alight her fire?
A gangling youth, in drunken revelry,
whose burly frame and ready laugh inspire
admiring looks, he has no cavalry
to defend him from her array of charms,
her cleavage weaponry, dress slit to thigh.
He buys her drinks, she snuggles in his arm,
she kisses him, the spider has her fly.
The night progresses with this happy pair
oblivious to anything but them,
the hubbub all around, the jealous stare,
the jostling crowd in closing-time mayhem.
Who is the winner in this game of chance
the one who lusts, the one who seeks romance?

A Highland Vagabond

The one who lusts, the one who seeks romance?
Ye think I'm saft because I'm frae the north.
Aye weel I ken yer game, bit whit's the chance
o getting sic a lassie, an in truth
a fancy rinnin hauns aroun yer curves.
A'd be dytit tae let this night slip bye,
ye've whispered yes, an aw yer likes and loves,
ten meenits hame an in ma bed ye'll lie,
a'll show ye whit a highlander can do.
We'll wake the morrow wi a thousand sighs,
a'll say they words o love as if they're true,
hae me anither day between yer thighs.
Sic are the wounds and scars o shallow lusts,
if flesh is all we have, flesh turns to dust.

The dinner party 1

If flesh is all we have, flesh turns to dust,
with final course, Waitrose Haloumi cheese,
this topic will be awkward for Louise
and Jim has almost choked upon a crust.
They think I'm unaware of how they lust.
I have the photograph, she's on her knees
her plump breasts swing, her mouth ready to please.
My bastard husband has betrayed my trust,
a fool would recognise a man on heat.
I saw the signs, there have been other times,
our marriage had so many ups and downs,
well now the sin he sows, is what he'll reap.
I will be rich, to paraphrase Sondeheim's
sad lyrics of regret, they are the clowns.

The dinner party 2

Sad lyrics of regret, I am the clown
for flesh is all I have, flesh turns to dust.
She hums that song, a hollow tone, she must
have found out. I see Jim squirm and frown.
She serves Halloumi cheese, I wish I could
throw it in her face. This is so unjust,
every mouthful chokes and I feel the thrust
of her laughter, she says the courts have stood
up for wronged wives, the innocent party.
I am a fool, I only wanted thrills,
Jim said his wife would look away, didn't care.
He was rich and I loved playing tarty
as long as he was there to pay the bills.
I say get stuffed, I'm out and down the stair

A Student Rants in University Avenue

I say get stuffed, I'm out and down the stair.
Ye've given me a fail, I pay yer fees
no jist fir drink and birds, I'm expectin mair
from you. Tae say ma poetry doesnae please
I'll take, but no this forcing me tae be
some shadow o an awd bitch on the shelf.
I'm young an in ma prime, can ye no see
I dinnae want tae write jist like yer self.
Ye pointed oot my rhymes are somewhit bland,
ye say ye cannae understand ma voice.
Weel maybe yous the wan who needs a hand,
for I'm the future, an ye have no choice,
the old rules are in flight, they've had their day,
these lines ye hate are whit I have tae say.

In University Gardens a Tutor Replies

These lines I hate are what you have to say,
but is it worth the saying that's my point,
writing is a difficult interplay
of thought, emotion, your lines disappoint
me. Read widely, find your inspiration
in every day things, in people that you meet.
Give what I tell you due consideration,
success and failure a poet has to greet
with equal equanimity, your task
is not to pander to my tutor's view,
you do not listen, ranting when I ask
for a poem that is not glib but true.
Do not despair, one day it will come right
and we will share some wine, get drunk one night.

The Professor's Party

And we will share some wine, get drunk one night,
that mix of West End chic, plebian rough,
student and I putting the world to right
in a Hillhead garden, this is the stuff
of nightmares. Over there a couple kiss,
he's old enough to know the time and place
for such displays of lust, and it's not this,
and I am struggling to avoid disgrace,
this lad is hot, his poetry is crap
but look, slim hips, those shoulders and that grin,
he flicks his hair and has me in a flap,
my muse capitulates says, sin, sin, sin.
Thus she takes without apology,
for he will star in her anthology.

The Professor's Party 2

For I will star in her anthology,
I'll get a First frae her, dinnae doubt it.
I'm bloody guid in bed, an ken that's whit
she's got in mind, see yon biology
makes me another Byron or a Hughes.
This night she'll find ma poetry improve
wi every gentle touch, my every move.
It will be a scandal, I'll make the news,
breakin hearts, ma earthy verses winnin
a reputation as a new age man.
I'll grow wi poems of love's discontents,
on how I thought her great from the beginnin.
To have success, I had tae bring a plan,
oh, misses, from yon West-end tenements.

The Truce

Oh, missus, from yon West-end tenements
ye thought tae show me up before yer mates
I wis brighter than yer tricks. Wi kinder fates
I rose above yer privileged contempt.
But now I'm heading home wi all I sought
let's condemn those petty squabbles tae the past.
Animosity is poison, should not last.
Call a truce to our battles, they matter naught
in the great scheme of things. The day is fine,
see young and old parading on the street.
Before I go, a last attempt to please.
If you would agreed to spend a little time
with me; let me buy you a parting treat,
and like yon couple, sit drinking herbal teas

With Power comes betrayal

Never talk to strange men

my father said never talk to a policeman
keep your own counsel and walk on by
and teenage me so righteous and unworldly
was surprised probably the first time I began
to question his advice those steps into adulthood
learning to fall and rise and make mistakes
wander alleyways how hope hate love worry makes
for white and black merging into grey so I would
come to understand that his advice was right
authority will forge your truth to their need
you are expendable to their good their devil
and now I coorie doon keep out of sight
the wisdom of three monkeys is my creed
hear no evil see no evil speak no evil

*

Hear no evil see no evil speak no evil
when I met a London police sergeant
full of prejudice and so arrogant
I hid a scream remained so civil
he boasted that he knew who was guilty
always fixed it for the right decision
his chilling grin without contrition
like an ancient lord demanding fealty
sent a chill deep deep into my soul
I let him charge along on his high horse
shook my head and said I could not help
he looked at me as if to swallow whole
then stood grunted left with a glowering curse
like a brute kicks a puppy to hear it yelp

*

like a brute kicks a puppy to hear it yelp
the powerful believe all they do is right
no one must challenge their use of might
keep your head down avoid the legal skelp
of laws provided to ensure they win
sub-postmasters jailed directors honoured
revellers fined and politicians exonerated
need help from the state a cardinal sin
it is you the rules are meant to destroy
head over the parapet they'll shoot it off
keep quiet keep servile while you plan
how to survive gather strength employ
the silent crowds who have had enough
of this you must never talk to a policeman

Milton Keynes UK
Ingram Content Group UK Ltd.
UKHW010559110124
435849UK00004B/96